R.A.A.P.

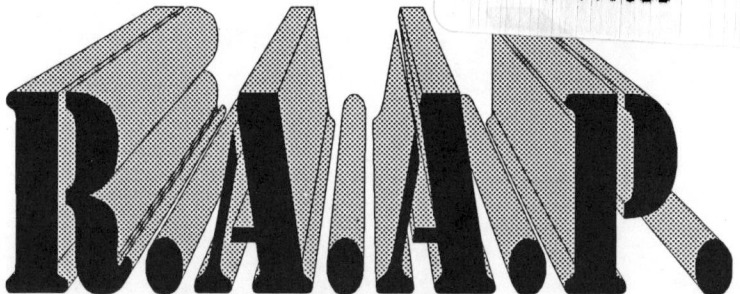

R.A.A.P.
Responsibilitating African American Parents

BY
IDA V. ST. HILL

PUBLISHED BY
SIMOUNTAINHILL
LAKE GROVE, N. Y.

Copyright © 1993 by Ida V. St. Hill

All rights reserved. No part of this book may be reproduced or transmitted in any form, including mechanical, electronic, photocopying, recording, or any information storage and retrieval system without prior written permission from the author.

Photo Credits . . . . The Family
Edited by Joyce Johnson
Cover Illustration by William Eris Johnson
Printed in the United States of America
by Minuteman Press of Selden
Published by Simountainhill Publishers
ISBN 0-9640736-0-9

DEDICATION

*T*his book is dedicated to my four children - Gillie, Gayle, Greg, and Darryl; to my Step-daughter, Denise; to all their children, and to all their children yet to be born. I also dedicate this book to all the Parents who entrusted their children's early education to my care, throughout the 24 years I spent in the classroom. I would also like to express my deepest gratitude to my own parents, who as my role models, instilled within me a sense of value, self-esteem and faith in a Living God. And finally, I would like to dedicate this book to the enduring spirit of My People - a People whose roots began with the seeds of the Kings and Queens of Africa - a People who survived the Middle Passage and the institution of slavery and bigotry - to stand on the threshold of the 21st Century. I see hope for the future of my People each time I look into the eyes of my grandchildren.

> "And you shall know the truth,
> and the truth shall set you free."
> -John 8: 32 -

ACKNOWLEDGMENTS

I would like to express my sincere and deepest gratitude to all of the special people in my life who encouraged me to write and publish this book. Special thanks go to my children - Darryl and Gayle - for their time and patience while teaching me the language of the computer, without which this book would never have been completed. And to the following people who have shared their thoughts and ideas with me, and contributed in no small way, towards the completion of this book - I give my heartfelt thanks: Doris Boyd, Kenneth Clark, Lenora Chapman, Bernie McMahon, Bill Gatlin, Esterphine Greene, Lloyd Bernard, Betty Hodges, Charlie Vaughan, Mia Isaac, Xavier Molina, Gilbert Fountain Jr., Deborah Lawson, Joyce Johnson and Gertrude Blackwell.

Although the incidents in this book are descriptions of actual incidents taken from real experiences throughout my lifetime, the names have been changed and fictionalized, and any similarity to persons, living or dead is purely coincidental.   I. V. S.

Contents

DEDICATION i
ACKNOWLEDGMENTS ii
INTRODUCTION 7
SOUL FOOD 17
R. A. T. S. 21
    ■RACISM 22
    ■ANGER 26
    ■TEMPTATION 27
    ■SCHOOLS 28
GETTING A "G. E. D." 30
    ■GOD 31
    ■EDUCATION 34
    ■DIET 61
LOVE = TIME ! TIME = LOVE 66
LANGUAGE 72
DISCIPLINE 83
SEXUAL RESPONSIBILITY 90
SOLUTIONS 106
LETTER TO GOD 110

INTRODUCTION

"There are two people in this world who can change the direction it is going - YOU and ME!"

When I was a little girl, I remember reading a story about the animals who thought the sky was falling. As the animals approached a little bird lying in the road on his back with his feet up in the air. They asked him what was he doing. The little bird answered, "I'm holding the sky up." All the animals laughed at him. "You expect to hold up the sky with those little legs?" The bird answered: "Everyone's got to do the best he can with what he's got."

The sky is falling on our kids, and I'm doing the best I can with what I've got - I've got the power of the word! With the help of a merciful God, I got my 4 children to the other side - (past the age of 21) and now I'm here to help you get yours through. We Parents are the first line of defense in keeping the sky from falling on them - not the government - not the schools - not the Church. It is our direct responsibility to keep that sky from swallowing up our children.

While I am concerned about the sky falling on all of the children of our nation, I am most concerned with the hostile environment in which our African American children must live, learn and grow. It will take the courage, strength and the good graces of God for us to lift this burden off of the backs of our children. If we, as Parents, don't assume that responsibility, our race faces extinction by the year 3000. Survival of the fittest is the law of the Animal Kingdom, (of which we are a part).

From time to time I might generalize, but the ideas in this book are my opinions (I'm sure not mine alone), but I don't claim to speak for the whole, about the whole. I speak to and about those of you whose actions or non-actions affect the whole.

I wrote this book because I, as an African-American Parent and Teacher have observed a decline in the moral atmosphere in our communities and schools. The decline can only be directly coming from the home, first and foremost. We like to point fingers by blaming the government (they don't send enough money to the cities), by blaming the schools (they don't teach), by blaming the "system" (whatever that is), but as we point the finger of blame, the other four fingers point back at the ones who are ultimately responsible - We Parents! Parents are the first line of defense in this war against R. A. T. S. - (Racism, Anger, Temptation, and Schools that don't educate.) If we don't stand guard at the door, the R. A. T. S. will get in and devour our kids. If we don't put the protection of self-love and self-discipline around our kids, they will be devoured by R. A. T. S. in our streets, and in our schools.

The first step in any Twelve Step Program for addiction is the admittance of one's own responsibility - owning the problem. If you are the problem , you have to fix the problem. As any therapist will tell a person with a relationship problem, you have to do the changing before you can expect anyone else to change. You must change your attitude! Change your mindset! Change the way you speak! Change the way you act! Believe me, other people will change the way they act and speak about you! And change your sense of responsibility! It takes a person with vision to accept this responsibility for change. Change is often fraught with uncertainty and pain. It's painful to look in the mirror and not like what you see. It's more painful to own up to the truth of what you see and when we look at our collective selves in the mirror of time we must realize that where we go from here depends upon You and Me.

I wrote this book because I recognized the fact that there is no hate group spawned by ignorance in this country doing more damage to our people than what we are doing to ourselves. KKK bigotry and hatred is spawned and fed by ignorance. Just as the African Holocaust robbed and raped Africa of its manhood and womanhood for four centuries, enslaving the healthiest and strongest, so is there a present-day holocaust in the streets and schools of our communities - a holocaust that is enslaving and destroying the healthiest and strongest of our young African-American men.

I wrote this book because I believe our kids are frantically begging us to STOP THEM! Their actions speak loud and clear that they're on a runaway train that's heading for the Cliff of Death! They're screaming at us, " Stop Us! Stop Us! Pull the Emergency Brake! Do Something! Do Anything! But Please, Stop Us!" The disaster that is happening in our communities, can only be stopped by you and me - the Parents, by pulling the Emergency Brake before disaster hits us all!

I wrote this book because I don't hear the same outrage coming from our African-

American communities when one of our own young men kills another one of our own, as I hear when a "Blue-Coat" -(policeman - the color of skin is irrelevant) kills one of our own. All too often the one killed is an innocent child, in what is now referred to as "drive-bys." Hate groups can't accomplish their goal (our annihilation) without help. Each time you read about another drive-by, the killer should get a check from a member of the KKK. He's done their job.

I wrote this book because I can't remain silent anymore. "Silence gives consent" I can't remain silent when I see our African American children coming to school angry and defiant and showing no respect for discipline or authority. I can't remain silent when I see entire neighborhoods under siege by these same children who reduce their parents and teachers to such "burn-out" terms, as "he should do this" and "they should've done that". "Shoulds" and "should'ves" are nothing more than "wish-lists".

"Lloyd should do his homework." ("I wish Lloyd would do his homework.") Whose responsibility is it to see that Lloyd does his homework?

"Penny shouldn't go to that unsupervised party." ("I wish Penny wouldn't go to that unsupervised party.") Whose responsibility is it to see that Penny does not go to that unsupervised party?

Six year old Irene stays up late at night watching adult - (and many times, violent) movies. "I know she shouldn't be watching these movies, but she won't go to bed when she should." Whose responsibility is it to see that Irene goes to bed at HER bedtime hour and not her parent's? And whose responsibility is it to protect Irene from polluting her mind with the corrupt messages of adult TV?

"The government should"; "The schools should"; "The parents should"; "The children shouldn't" and most often heard, "They should" (who's "THEY"?) become "wish - lists" - but these words make us immobile and slow to act. "Shoulds" and "should'ves" tend to release us from responsibility. When we change these "shoulds" and "should'ves" to "It's my responsibility" then we will act accordingly and take charge of our own destiny and it teaches our children that they are in charge of their own destiny. That's called EMPOWERMENT!

    I wrote this book with the vision and hope that someone will read these words and save a child at risk - a child who may one day become a Nobel Peace Prize winner or save the world from total destruction; or a child who may become an explorer - not of outer space but of the inner space of the body, mind and soul; or a child who may discover the cure for AIDS or Cancer or world hunger. The person I admire most after my parents is Harriet Tubman, who said "I'd rather die free on my feet than live as a slave on my knees".

    After spending 24 years teaching young African American children the "4 R's" - 'Reading, 'Riting, 'Rithmetic and Responsibility, I came to the realization that despite what I taught in the classroom, the Parents of these children had the greatest impact on their lives; and the awesome responsibility was ultimately theirs. I am also convinced that no outside pressure is greater than that of a loving, nurturing home, where the children grow in self-discipline and self-worth as a result of a strong parental value system.

For these reasons, I have written this book.

Before I go any further let me explain here, that for every "He" in this book, there is a "She"; for every "him" in this book, there is a "Her". So that I don't sound redundant, please read he/she and him/her each time you see the male pronoun. What's sauce for the goose (female) is sauce for the gander (male) - right?

SOUL FOOD

"Every child is born with the message that God is not yet discouraged of Man"

- Tagore

A child comes into the world after spending nine months in the warm fluid of an amniotic sac, nourished passively through the umbilical cord attached to his mother. Before conception is the time to prepare your body (female) and sperm (male) for the "miracle" of a healthy baby. The pregnancy period is even more critical. Would you give your baby drugs and vodka? Would you give your baby a cigarette? For all of you who said "No of course not!" And drank smoked and used drugs during your pregnancy, answer that question again. Your baby's body, his teeth, his bones, and most importantly, his brain is developing through that nine month period. Think of the consequences of "using" while you are pregnant. (By the way, you guys don't get off so easily either in the responsibility of making a baby.) If you are using drugs, drinking or smoking, those sperm cells you're shooting off are also defective, consequently your baby may be defective from conception.

I believe that a person's soul is not in the heart but in the brain. (Can anyone disprove my theory?) And this brain becomes the control center of the person's entire life - from conception to the grave. Remember that, future parents when you have the temptation to smoke that joint, crack, cigarette or take that drink - at the point when you have absolute control over the entire life of another human being - your child. And when that child is born, you might not realize it right away but you have planted the seed that will change the chemistry of his brain, of his spirit, and eventually, it becomes a hole in his soul. And all you see is a little beautiful baby.

After your baby is born he is completely dependent on you for nourishment. Just as he is dependent upon you for nourishment of his body, he is also completely dependent upon you for nourishment of his soul. As you feed him milk and baby food, you must also feed him a sense of security and values. This nourishment takes many forms - talking to, holding, hugging, giving attention to, cuddling and giving him YOUR TIME. I think it is so important to give a child your TIME, I spend a whole chapter on it - (See, "Love = Time") . You notice I don't say give him "Love" because every parent says " I love my baby" and then you see parents either ignoring or neglecting him, and in more serious cases, abusing him. Love is Not Enough! You have to FEEL love, and TOUCH love, and SEE love, and HEAR love, and SMELL love, and TASTE love. That takes TIME!

During the years I spent in the classroom, I recognized so many children starving for the touch of another human warm body; starving for affection and attention. I counselled many of the parents of these children and told them to give them more undivided time; to talk to them and to give them the security of their love - what I call " Food for the Soul". What a difference I noticed in these children after these parent-teacher talks! The children seemed calmer, more disciplined and more ready to learn. We've all seen the eyes of a child in Somalia who is starving for food. If you look into the eyes of a child starving for affection and attention, you see almost the same kind of look - except in this case, it's a starvation of the soul - look.

R. A. T. S.

Racism Anger Temptation Schools

The moral decay of this country seems to be following the same moral decay, social and political decline as the empires of the Greeks, Romans and Egyptians. None of the great empires were overthrown from outside forces. They became their own worst enemy and the decline of their great empires started from the moral seeds decaying in the hearts and souls of its people. Its our responsibility - not solely ours but PRIMARILY ours, nevertheless, to eradicate our neighborhoods of this scourge because no one else is going to come to our rescue. It is our responsibility first to immunize our children against measles, smallpox, diphtheria and R. A. T. S. Our children must confront R. A. T. S. everyday that they walk out of the house and I'm not talking about the nasty creatures that scurry around the sewer systems of our cities. I refer to Racism, Anger, Temptation and Schools that don't Educate.

RACISM comes in many shapes, sizes and colors. Racism is blatant and loud; Racism is subtle and underhanded. Racism can destroy - both the hated and the vessel that carries the hate - the racist. Racism can be the written law or it can be unwritten, but the law can't unwrite the racism in the soul.

Racism has a way of working itself from the inside to the outside as you see every time you see a cross burning event; and it has a way of working itself from the outside to the inside as you see each time you see brothers killing brothers and calling each other by the same degrading word of the racist - "Nigger" and disrespecting their own sisters by calling them "Bitches".

And racism is always ugly! Look at the faces of the racists and bigots on the TV talk shows. Maybe I'm reading this into their faces but their faces always seem tight and pursed and **UGLY**. Racism can either do one of two things to oppressed people. Racism can unite a people together in such a strong bond that they overcome the racism. (Read the history of India and their protest movement against racism under the leadership of Mohandas Gandhi - called "Mahatma" - "Great Soul"). Or racism can separate a People and make them feel helpless and live the life of the eternal Victim. Which have we become?

In 1895 Booker T. Washington said in his speech "We can be as separate (and useless) as the fingers spread open on your hand. Ball your fingers into a fist and they act as one; acting as one unit is essential to mutual progress". I've always sung the song "We Shall Overcome" with the more determined words - "We Will Overcome!" To me, it was more decisive and positive because we Will overcome just by the strength of our Will. That gives us the ability and the knowledge of Power. That is EMPOWERMENT!

When we allow ourselves and our children to constantly blame the racist society in which they must live for all the miseducation, joblessness and mistreatment, we allow them to be stuck in the quicksand of the Eternal Victim, and they begin to see everything from the victim's perspective. Instead of looking forward they are always looking back.

I'm reminded of the story of the man who was constantly involved in automobile accidents. He finally went to an expert and asked him why he was always getting into these crashes with his car. The expert said "Let's go for a drive and I'll observe your driving." After they returned, (from yet another accident), the expert said to him, "I see why you're always crashing into things. You're constantly looking through your rear-view mirror."

That mirror is what I call a "Victim's Mirror". We must never forget the past and the holocaust that stripped a whole continent of its best resource - its best people. But we cannot allow ourselves to keep looking at life through a mirror that only reflects the past.

The only way I see that we can overcome racism is through education. Let's sing one of those "We Shall (WILL) Overcome" verses with "WE WILL EDUCATE". Parents, educate yourself, educate your children because those who don't get an education become the prisoners of tomorrow – literally and figuratively. 90 % of the prison population are High School dropouts. The prisons of this country are filled with our bright but uneducated children and the children who have allowed themselves to be enslaved by drugs and alcohol.

    I often wondered what my six year old students visualized when I tried to teach them what slavery was. I gave them the picture of people with chains around their wrists and ankles. And how slaves today have invisible chains around their brains. I told them that anyone who doesn't drink from the Fountain of Education is putting themselves in jeopardy of becoming enslaved. And people who use drugs are growing cobwebs in their brains; those cobwebs surround their brains so they can't think and learn. And before they know it there are chains around their brains. And they have become another slave!

ANGER comes from the seeds of despair and hopelessness. Anger comes from fear and uncertainty. Angry children come from angry homes where parents are angry at the inequities of life, at the "system" and at God Himself. Angry children come to school unsure of today with no hope for tomorrow. They have no security blanket around them that protects them from fear. The rage that our Middle School and High School teachers face everyday, is the outgrowth of this fear.

So many of our children are coming to school with the fear of being shot along the way, or even once arriving safely at school, being shot while at school. It is estimated that one in five students are carrying weapons to, from and in school. No wonder our kids are suffering from the same trauma of our returning Vietnam Veterans—what psychoanalysts are calling "Post-traumatic Syndrome". Go into any inner-city school in this country and ask the children how many of them have heard shots fired in their neighborhoods, or know someone who has been shot. Can you imagine a child sitting in a classroom, trying to pay attention to his lessons, when he is looking out of windows into the same "R. A. T." infested streets he must negotiate to get back home? Anger is one letter short of Danger - and to some of our children, they're both the same.

TEMPTATION is everywhere, no matter where you live. But to our kids, temptation is right outside our doors, on the doorstep, on the street corner, and in the schools. Temptation takes the form of a BMW driven by a drug dealer or a pimp. Temptation comes in the form of "Best" friend trying to convince your child to shoplift, to smoke a joint, or to have unprotected, irresponsible sex. It's what we call "Peer Pressure".

A child who has self-esteem, self-worth and self-discipline will not fall into this Peer Pressure rathole; but it is our responsibility as parents to begin instilling this sense of self value from birth. A child who knows he is valued and loved unconditionally; a child who has internalized his own code of discipline will build up a moral immune system that no amount of Peer Pressure will penetrate.

SCHOOLS that don't educate are such an important issue to deal with, I've committed a whole chapter on it. (See the chapter on Education.) I've already made it quite clear that we WILL overcome - only when we recognize how vital it is to be an educated People. So sing with me: "We Will Educate".

Parents, there will never be anything you do in your life more important, more rewarding or harder; there will never be a responsibility greater than getting your child safely across the sea of R. A. T. S. to the other side of 21 years of age.
And believe me, it ain't easy! Picture yourself as a Knight - (or "Knightress"?) in a suit of armor, with a sword in your hand, and your kids under your arm, as you fight off the sea of R. A. T. S. that's trying to devour your kids! Whatever sacrifices you have to make

along the way, make them. Be determined to make it! Determined people say, " I Will!" Lazy people say, " I Could!" Stupid people say "I Can't!"

Remember, your child is God's Gift to you. What you make of him is your Gift to God.

GETTING A "G. E. D."

❧

It is for the "soul, mind and body" of which I refer when I say give your child his "G. E. D." I don't mean getting a High School Equivalence Diploma; I mean give your child

    God for his spiritual life,
    Education for his mental life, and a good
    Diet for his physical life.

GOD

"No God - No Peace : Know God - Know Peace"

No matter what religion you are (or aren't), it is your responsibility as a parent to give your child a spiritual life; a faith in a Power greater than himself. Whether your "Good" Book be The Bible, The Koran, or The Torah, the fundamental message is the same. And God certainly must have meant for us to treat our neighbor especially good if He said to love them as we love ourselves. Who among us doesn't love ourselves best? Well, I guess there are some, Huh? When you see children who have no love for their brothers they in turn have no love for themselves. If they feel their lives have no value, it becomes easy for them to feel that your life has no value and it becomes easy to pick up a gun and kill you. The fear of punishment or even the fear of death - whether their own or someone else's death is not present in their value system.

When they are little, children learn to say the "God is Good, God is Great" prayer before meals, and the "Now I Lay Me Down To Sleep" prayer before bedtime. But they never see their parents on bended knee in prayer, or reading the Holy Book at home, on a regular basis. Spirituality is the foundation of the laws of right and wrong; it is the core of the conscience, the essence of morality, the "wholeness" of the soul. I don't refer to organized religion, because each religion considers its roadmap to God and the hereafter, the best, and in some cases, the only route, and only they hold the "passport." I refer to that spiritual existence to which we all strive - no matter which religion - Love of God and Love of Neighbor. It's impossible to love one and hate the other. Parents, put God first in your life; your children will do the same!

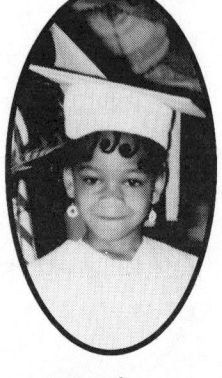

The Road to Freedom!

EDUCATION

"Education is our passport to the future, for tomorrow belongs to the people who prepare for it today" -
Malcolm X

You are your child's first and best teacher. From infancy, you are teaching your child to say "Please" and "Thank You" and how to hold a fork. It is your responsibility to see that your child is prepared for school - that he is ready to learn. Remember, learning doesn't always come naturally. Children must learn how to learn. Therefore, you have to prepare your child for the structure and discipline of the classroom. Always speak positively and often of the rewards of education; motivate him for success. Continuous praise is a great motivator. I've never seen a child that didn't put just a pound more of effort into a task with just an ounce more of praise.

"Excellence is attained only when we push ourselves to our maximum potential beyond the expected goal. To do less allows mediocrity to take its place..."

EXPECTATIONS

According to the laws of aerodynamics, the bumble bee can't fly. His body is too heavy for his wings. But he expects to fly and despite those laws he flies anyway!

With the proper motivation from his parents, a child enters kindergarten and first grade - (nowadays its pre-K), eager to learn and expecting to learn. Unless the motivation and encouragement is sustained daily by the parent, by the 3rd or 4th grade, the child has "dropped out". "Drop-outs have no expectations. A child who is continually told he can't achieve will not achieve. There are recognizable signs of a potential drop-out. "Does not work up to his potential"; "easily distracted", "daydreams" etc. are report card comments that signal a potential drop-out. If a child is not challenged because "He can't", it's your responsibility to find out why. A lot of children mentally drop out of school because they find no challenging interest there. It's definitely not because they're stupid!

    Equally as important as the child's expectations of himself are the expectations of his teachers. Many years ago, I observed three different classrooms in another school district. All of the classes were on the 4th grade level. Since tracking was used - a system of placing children in classes according to functioning and/or reading level (called homogeneous grouping), I visited a 4A (1) - a class of high expectation; a 4A (2) - a class of moderate expectation and a 4A (3) class - a class of very little expectation. When I visited the 4A (1) class, the teacher was throwing out questions to the students so rapidly, I even had trouble keeping up and was quite impressed with the level of knowledge and excitement in the class. These children were being challenged; they were alert, quick-minded and interested. In the 4A (2) class the children were working on assignments that didn't seem as challenging or interesting. When I sat in on the 4A (3) class I almost fell asleep. The teacher droned on and on and on, almost in a monotone, speaking ever so slowly that I found it difficult to connect thoughts and purpose for the lesson- (if there was a lesson). After class this teacher smiled at me and said "The children you just observed are slow and incapable of learning. They live in the Project". Well, it became clear that little was expected of these children; they were unchallenged, disinterested and undisciplined. And this teacher tried to justify her lack of enthusiasm because "These kids live in the Project" I later found out that most of the children in the other classes came from the same Project.

Have you ever been told that you would never amount to anything? Well, tell your kids that if they are ever told that to remember the Best Revenge is Success! A colleague of mine had been told that 20 years ago. She made a special trip back to that school recently to see that teacher with her PhD. in hand!

Many school districts have the same type tracking system, but now we have a hydra- (that's the mythological multi-headed monster) called Special Education. Special Ed. was created for those children who are handicapped - either physically, mentally, or emotionally. So many of our African-American children have been placed in these Special Ed. classes because of their behavior. A disruptive child in a classroom quickly becomes a candidate for the Special Ed. program. And then the child begins to justify his behavior - "Everybody acts this way" - and he seeks attention and validation by becoming the class clown or by becoming angry and sullen and defiant. And he has become another drop - out, not only from school, but also from society.

Parents, beware of these tactics. I'm not saying its easy to teach a class of 30-35 students with disruptive children in the classroom, but if you get reports that your child is being disruptive, get up to school and investigate. Sit in the classroom from time to time and observe the atmosphere in that classroom. Join Parent Advocate groups, and discuss how you can help your child be more self-disciplined. (If you don't have a Parent Group, start one). Ask the teacher to give anecdotal notes about your child's behavior. I know of one teacher who put the tape recorder on to record a child's behavior in the classroom when the parent didn't believe her child was acting up. Wow, was that parent in for a shock! And was that kid in for a "serious attitude-changing session"! It worked!

Parents, you have the power to change what goes on at your child's school. You've heard of Peer Pressure. Well, you have no idea what power you have until you use Parent Pressure! As long as you remain complacent and uninvolved, things will remain the same, and everyone will just continue to complain about the "System".

Do you think our children are less intelligent than the children of other races? I think not. Poverty may be rampant in our poor, roach and rat infested neighborhoods, but their is no poverty of intelligence there. There is no legislation that can prevent Poverty of the Soul. Poverty of the pocketbook is the result of poor expectations and poor education. The result of poor nutrition is poor health; poor health results in poor school attendance; poor school attendance results in poor education. It's a vicious cycle but Parents, you can break the cycle. Join forces with other parents and break the cycle of poverty. Educate yourself and educate your children. Use any means possible to see that your children break out of this Cycle of Poverty.

That means you have to unite! You all have the same purpose, the same economic conditions, the same goals - and that is the education of your children. You cannot do it alone. Form a Parent Council or a Parent Advocate group in your neighborhood whereby you have a networking between Parents who work outside the home and Parents who don't work outside the home, who can visit school a little more often. Make it a network that keeps ALL Parents informed of school related problems and activities.

I'm reminded of the story I told my former 1st graders every year when introducing the concept of Martin Luther King's speech to the people of Montgomery, Alabama at the beginning of the bus boycott there in 1955. I asked the children to name one of the most powerful animals in the world. Of course, answers such as "Elephants", "Whales" "Man" were the responses I got. Imagine the look on their faces when I told them one of the most powerful animals in the world was the little tiny ant! I explained that one tiny ant can't do the job but when thousands of ants work together, they can build mountains, destroy mountains, and even move mountains. That's one of the greatest lessons I received from Rev. Dr. Martin Luther King. He taught us that all the people of Montgomery had to suffer the hardships brought on by boycotting the buses for almost an entire year; or the boycott would have failed. And perhaps we might still be sitting at the back of the bus by law. Thank you, Rosa Parks for your tired feet!

And Thank you, Montgomery, for your sacrifice!

So, Parents, put this book down right now and pick up that phone and call somebody and begin a PARENT PRESSURE NETWORK on your block or in your school district. Know what is going on in the school so you and the other Parents can make educated decisions. It's Parent Pressure against Peer Pressure!

Network with the teachers so they know what you and the other parents want or don't want for your children. Insist that standards of behavior and discipline be maintained in the school. Demand standards of safety in the school. Find out what kind of food they are feeding your children in breakfast and lunch programs. Don't just read the menu, check the freshness of the food and how it's being served. Join forces with other parents and with the teachers. Make the rules of expected behavior and the consequences that go with breaking the rules, together.

Children must have a sense of responsibility for arriving at school on time and if the rules have already been set in place by both parents and teachers, they will know that they will suffer the consequences for their tardiness. I see children nowadays strolling into school late, like they are out for a stroll in the park. The consequences of such indifference must be instantly dealt with or children will feel that rules are not to be taken seriously. If the school authorities do not enforce the rules, it is your responsibility as Parents to see that they do. Children who get away with breaking school rules, lose respect for authority, and begin to believe that rules can be ignored. As they grow older, rules become laws, and they see no reason why those can't be ignored and broken, either! Be alert! Use your Parent Pressure. It works!

    Some children come to school with no parental discipline and find comfort and security in a structured, well disciplined classroom. Once they know where the boundaries are they adjust quite well and actually thrive in such an atmosphere. I've heard parents say that they don't feel welcome in their child's school. If you feel this way bring it up at one of your meetings - and by the way - Don't say you don't have time for meetings. Your child goes to school for ten months out of the year. You can make ten meetings in a year (one a month). I have seen children as young as 4 and 5 years old coming to school by themselves on the first day of school. When I asked "Where's Mommy?" Answer : "Home in bed". Sometimes the entire year went by and I didn't see a child's parent at school. That's why I often made home visits to find out why the child was having attendance problems or other problems at school. Much too often I found a Lazy Parent who just didn't care enough to see that the child got up on time in the mornings, or that the child arrived safely to and from school.

   Too many of our children are walking unsafe streets alone. Every year at least one child in our school district was hit by a car going to or from school. It is your responsibility to know where your child is at all times.

   If you have a Parent network in place you

can make better choices when Debbie asks "Can I stay out until midnight. Doris' mother lets her stay out until midnight". Know Doris' mother and find out what the real deal is. When you have a Parent Network in place you will know, what she allows Doris to do, or not do. It will probably turn out that Doris' mother doesn't let her stay out either. But if she does, just remind her that every new baby comes with a price tag. The price tag is RESPONSIBILITY ! Some parents give the bill to the government or to a social agency. Some parents give the bill to grandparents and other family members. Some parents begin to pay for several years - while their babies are little and cute, and lose the price tag after the baby becomes a not-so-cute kid. And some parents continue to pay the price in 7, 665 installments - (the number of days it takes to get them safely to age 21). Tell her you're on installment #5, 175 and you've invested too much time, and "RESPONSIBILITATING" to cash the policy in yet.

And Parents, Ban Curfew! That's right I said Ban Curfew! When that 30 second blurb comes on your TV that says; "It's 10 o'clock. Do you know where your children are?", can you answer "Yes!" with confidence? When I see children (some as young as 8 and 9 years old) running around the streets late at night, my first thought is "Where are their parents?"

When Hugh says, "Mom, I'm going out" It's Hugh's parents' responsibility to ask him if he has a destination, where that destination is, and when you expect him back from that destination. The time that he is due back depends upon the destination. If you've done your job up to this point then you will know his friends and hopefully his friend's parents. If you've done your job up to this point, you will not see your child hanging out on a street corner somewhere with unknown friends of questionable character. Ban the Curfew! Just know where your children are and you won't need a curfew. When there is a certain party on the agenda, again, curfew is not necessary if you know where the party is and if there will be parental supervision at the party. (Get it straight from the horse's (parent's) mouth.) Know how he will be getting to and from the party. (I spent many a sleepless night waiting for the phone to ring to come and pick up my kids from parties.)

And when you hear "my mother is so strict!" remind him that you are still on the 21 year installment plan of that Responsibility Policy that extends into life long coverage.

Back to the Schools! Insist upon being given an outline of what the course requires at the beginning of each semester. All children do not grow at the same rate; neither do they learn at the same rate. Teachers who keep their parents informed just confirm what the parent already knows when report card time comes. Parents should not be surprised when they read their child's report card. Look at the grade in "Effort" first. All the other grades are the icing on the cake. The grade in Effort is the cake. With an "F" in effort you have a fallen unacceptable cake - no matter what the other grades are. "A" in effort signifies that the child did his very best. And that's all we can ask of our kids. An "F" in effort requires some intensive parent-child "discussion".

If academic problems arise, get your child extra help - from a tutor, from an Afterschool center, or from a local High School or College student. And if your child comes home saying he doesn't have any homework, find out why. Most school districts have a homework policy, so it's fair to say statements such as, "I don't have homework" or "I did my homework in school" needs to be checked out. Some teachers do not give homework because they do not want to take the time to check it. (And indeed, I've heard children complain that their teacher never checks their homework). If you hear such complaints, use your Parent Pressure and check out the real deal!

When you see your child going to and from school without books - and I see too many of our African American High School students walking without books - and the child says he doesn't carry books because he did his homework in school, use your Parent Pressure. Check out the real deal! If he actually did do his homework in school, HE'S NOT GETTING ENOUGH HOMEWORK! Insist he get more homework!

Parents help your child with homework as much as you can without actually "teaching" the lesson. Teachers are trained in the techniques of teaching, which you may or may not be familiar. If you see that your child has not grasped the concept of the lesson, notify the teacher that your little Junius doesn't understand the assignment or the concept of the lesson. Parents helping their children with homework is sometimes like a husband teaching his wife to drive. Whenever you feel like you are losing patience, remember, he is not deliberately acting like he's just undergone lobotomy surgery to spite you: just turn around and calmly write - L. G. M. P. ! (Lord, Give Me Patience!) Then turn around, smile, and either try to attack the problem again or write a note to the teacher that your little Junius just doesn't get it and ask her to review the concept again.

    Teachers enter our schools with the same degree of intolerance and prejudices as society as a whole. It is your responsibility to see that your child is treated with respect just as you teach your child to respect others. Teachers who say they don't see color, are either lying or are patronizing. When you look at my face you HAVE to see my color. I just don't want anyone seeing JUST my color and making preconceived assumptions about me based on just that information. Racism is the height of ignorance. You can hate me from a distance, long before you meet me face to face . Please, DO see my color! My people have been working on this tan for thousands of years and I'm proud of it. But don't see just my color and nothing else. Look into my heart and my soul. If you don't like what you see there, you have every right to dislike me.

    Teachers who accept disrespectful attitudes from our African American kids are also racists because that's all they expect of them. Instead of saying, "Isaiah, you can't wear that cap in the classroom," a teacher will ignore it because "that's to be expected". A racist teacher is one who "tolerates" the bad manners of her students because "that's to be expected of THEM"! When you see a student who is abusive to teachers, you can be sure that he has been allowed to get away with being defiant and rude for a long time.

Disrespect and verbal abuse don't appear instantly. It is fed as little seedlings of defiances - such as snatching books and papers from teachers; or sullen - "Why do I have to sit down? He's not sitting down." There are so many small defiant attitudes that if ignored, you'll find the little seedling has grown into an angry, hostile 6 ft. weed who's jumping up in the face of a teacher with a gun in his hand. "But that's to be expected of THEM!" And many of these racists are the same color as their students.

Then there are the teachers who are sensitive to the needs of their students without using the liabilities of their environment as handicapping excuses. These teachers recognize the fact that their students need structure and discipline along with T. L. C. (Tender Loving Care). They also recognize that because of the socialization process that they must go through to survive in a world of R. A. T. S., the needs of our children are different. They view the world differently. The child who acts the least lovable, is the child who is the most starved for love. The child who comes to school with the least discipline, is in need of a structured, disciplined classroom environment. I used to keep a "T. L. C." drawer in my desk. Along with "extra hug stickers", or "compliment" stickers, you could find anything from an apple or an orange to a clean pair of socks or a warm pair of gloves in that drawer.

Teachers who are sensitive to their students' needs, recognize and respect cultural differences. These teachers demand, expect and get the best from their students. And will accept no excuses for laziness or incompetence.

There is a current debate going on these days -whether African American students should only be taught by African American teachers - especially, our boys. As far as I'm concerned, color of skin does not make a teacher good, nor does it make him bad. A good teacher knows his subject, knows the best methods for getting the information from his brain to the brains of his students; always commands respect for himself and always demands respect for his students. There are millions of such teachers all around this country - and they come in all different colors, sizes and shapes.

I once asked a young man to name his best teacher and why he thought this teacher was his best. Without hesitation he named a Jewish teacher - Mr. Greenestein. When I asked him why he named this particular teacher he said, "Because Mr. Greenestein made me work, made me responsible for my own actions, and wouldn't let me get away with anything." So you see the color of one's skin doesn't make the difference...the color of one's soul makes the difference!

I do feel, however, the fact that Mr.

Greenestein was a man, might have been a factor. So many of our African American boys are being raised by single mothers, without any positive male role models in their lives. I would like to see more male teachers in classrooms - men of any race as long as they are sensitive to the needs of their students, giving them a sense of responsibility, discipline, and self-worth by the example they give - that of men of character, competence and self-respect.

Think back to the best teacher you had when you were in school. I'll bet that teacher was your hardest, (meanest, you thought at the time), strictest of them all. Because she -or he- wouldn't accept anything less than your very best!

If a teacher says she likes all of her students and treats them all the same, remember, children are people too and have personalities just as adults do. There certainly were some students that I disliked, but they were there to learn and I was there to teach them. And each of us had to respect the position of the other.

No one treats everybody the same. Everyone has a different perspective on life. The child who lives on the first floor and the child who lives on the tenth floor both look out at the same street, but they both look at it from different perspectives. Studies have been done that determined the order of birth gives children different perspectives of life. And they're all unique and all different!

If your child is having trouble learning, take advantage of the resources available in your school district. If your child has a learning disability, be sure your child is placed correctly. Be absolutely sure that tests prove there is a disability and that the "disability" is not laziness. Be sure to have your child's eyes tested and hearing checked by a doctor. I've seen quite a few changes in children's behavior and grades after getting glasses.

When problems arise at school that involves your child, you have a chain of command there to help you resolve it. Your first contact person is the teacher. Most problems can be resolved at this point. If after this contact, the problem still exists, the next person in the chain of command is the Principal. Ask for a meeting between yourself, the Principal, and the teacher. (Sometimes a classroom change is recommended at this point.) If after this meeting you still are not satisfied, make an appointment to see the Superintendent of your school district. After discussing the problem with the Superintendent, and you're still not satisfied, bring the issue up to the Board of Education.

When you have exhausted every avenue, and the problem still exists it's time to expose the issue in the Press. (I'll let you in on a little secret. School administrators hate negative press!) I've seen the results of such tactics. A parent who had been complaining about some girls who had her daughter terrified at school by constantly threatening her with physical harm, went to the press after following the chain of command and getting no results. Things changed pretty fast after the newspapers got the story! Parents, do whatever is necessary to protect your kids.

But, Parents, let me caution you who think your child is being "picked" on and you always find yourself up at school making excuses for your child's behavior. Take it from a parent, (me), who was called to the Principal's office more times than I would like to mention, that in most instances, the school staff is not out to "get" your kid. Stop making excuses for his behavior. (It's always someone else's fault.) Remember the "Victim's Mirror" I mentioned before? You will either make your child believe that he is always being victimized, therefore, he is always reacting to the victimizer, or he becomes a bully, knowing that his parents will defend his anti-social behavior. Teachers have the most unusual ability; they have the ability to grow 30 pairs of eyes - some in the back of their heads - and could teach Solomon a few tricks about wisdom and fairness when it comes to mediating and resolving conflicts in the classroom. When teachers use such terms as, "has difficulty getting along with peers"; "constantly getting into fights"; "uses inappropriate language and gestures"; "works best in small group setting"; what the teacher really means is your child is an obnoxious, offensive, bully; a social misfit, whose parents have not taught him basic socialization skills. The teacher can't tell you that in those words, without getting called on the carpet for it. For all of you who recognize your child from these descriptions, teach your child that he must first respect himself, and then he must show respect not only to his teacher, but also to all the assisting staff - from the aides to the custodial staff; and to his peers. A child who shows respect to those around him is unlikely to be involved in fights, and is usually well liked and respected by both peers and adults. A teacher is not given enough time in the day to teach your child all the socialization skills he needs and academics too. It is your responsibility to send a child to school ready to learn and any corrective measures in changing behavior and attitude is ultimately yours. Most teachers are hard working and conscientious, always looking for ways to ignite a thirst for learning in your children. I always said that I could lead a child to the water of knowledge; I might not be able to make him drink, but I sure could put the salt of success on his tongue that would make him thirsty.

So, parents, unless you suspect gross unfairness from your child's teacher or staff, stand with them and support them, and let your child know that his behavior away from home reflects how much you have been "responsibilitating" in the home.

Another parent I know, gave up a good job and moved from one part of the country to another, just to get her children away from a school environment that had her children in fear of their lives, everyday. She sacrificed her comfortable life, and all the things that the money from her job provided, to ensure her children a chance to grow up in a non - violent, safe, educationally sound school district. Parents, do whatever it takes to protect your children. That's Responsibilitating!

Education is a long term commitment. Those who have no vision of a tomorrow, or a hope for a future, can't see past today; therefore, they don't see the value and rewards of education. Begin preparing your child for College as soon as he's born. Start a Bond-a-Month habit. Instead of a toy for birthdays, buy him government bonds - label them - "College Bound Bonds!" Talk often to your child about his hopes and dreams. Start him off young, making plans for what he wants to be when he grows up. Whether he wants to be a nuclear physicist, a plumber, or a teacher, he has to put in at least 12 years of school to achieve his goal. Business school or College requires a longer commitment. Instead of "If you go to College, or trade school", speak in terms: "When you go to College, or trade school". Whatever you do, PREPARE YOUR CHILD TO WORK!

Wake up Parents! We're in a war and don't know it. The weapons are not nuclear bombs. The weapon is Education! The parent who has vision, plants seeds today for trees that will bear fruit for their grandchildren's grandchildren!

DIET

" Tell me what you eat and I'll tell you what you are. "

All of you young people , begin preparing your bodies now for that moment in time when sperm meets egg and a new human being begins forming and developing. The food you choose to eat , the nicotine you choose to smoke, the alcohol you choose to drink, or the drugs you choose to put into your system, -any one of these affect the sperm and the egg that will result in a fetus and after nine months, a baby. Once that baby is conceived, what the pregnant woman takes into her body, can be critical. If you are pregnant, and smoke, you put a cigarette in the hands of your baby. If you do drugs or alcohol, while pregnant, your unformed, developing baby is also doing drugs and drinking.

Babies who smoke and do drugs and drink, while they're building brain cells, are like building car engines with defective batteries. There's sure to be trouble down the road. These babies may not look brain damaged, but when they begin their academic life at school, it becomes quite apparent that their conceptual skills are way off center, and learning becomes difficult. And you have put your baby into the revolving doors of POVERTY.

Once your baby has arrived, he deserves the best start in life that is possible. As your baby grows, so does his control center – his brain. Through that brain, he must perceive everything in his world. If his brain is distorted, his perception of the world becomes distorted – and a hole silently begins to grow in his soul.

Parents, monitor what your children eat – especially during those first years when you have more control over what they eat. Fat cells begin developing during those years, and studies have proven that we African Americans are more susceptible to heart disease. The time to limit junk food is in these early years. Be sure you give them a good balanced diet everyday and make visits to fast food ("fat food") eateries infrequent.

Teach your children early in life what the "good" foods are and what foods to avoid. Keep less cookies and sweets in the house, and more fresh fruit and vegetables ready for snacks. Your children may not listen to everything you say, but they certainly will imitate what you do. If they see you stuffing yourself with sweets and "junk food", they will follow your example. I see too many young obese children, who are beginning to feel all the burdens that obesity brings. Their self-esteem is wrapped up in their image of themselves. The arteries they are clogging up may be the arteries to the heart, but they're also clogging up the arteries to their self-esteem.

It's your responsibility to send your child to school ready to learn. If there's no gas in the engine, the car can't go. Parents, send your child off to school with a healthy breakfast in the mornings. Many school districts around the country, have adopted breakfast programs where the children can get a meal before school begins. Take advantage of it if you can't provide it yourself. Lunch programs are also available. Since high amounts of fat and salt are deadly for us, especially, question the contents of the food they're feeding your child. Before long, I predict there will be Dinner Programs available, and another responsibility will be taken from Parents. And when our children grow up fighting obesity and hypertension, we will have one more "System" to blame – the Government Food Programs.

Mealtime is Family Togetherness Time. Few families these days eat together and when they do, there's another guest at the table, preventing conversation and sharing time – the T.V. Parents, INSIST that your family be together at the dinner table. You decide the time – 5 o'clock? – 6 o'clock? – 7 o'clock? Whatever is best for your family's busy schedule, call the time and insist that they appear at that time. The dinner hour may be the only time your family meets. This is sharing time - not only sharing a meal but sharing thoughts and ideas and happenings in each other's lives. Don't put it off until you're all strangers and don't know each other.

The next time you're wondering what to give as a wedding gift, give the newlyweds a guide to a "G. E. D." - a Bible, a Dictionary, and a Cookbook. It's a gift that will last a lifetime!

LOVE = TIME ! TIME = LOVE

> *The main ingredient of Love is Time!*

Think of Time as that little short line on your tombstone between your birthdate and your deathdate. That line represents your Life! No matter how long or short your life, you only get that short, little line. I imagine in the eons of Time that's what our lives are - a very, very short line in the memory of Time.

The time you spend with your child is the most valuable time of your life. Isn't it funny how we use the word - "spend"? We spend our most valuable assets - our money and our time. You could spend a million dollars on your kid and it wouldn't equal one minute spent on your kid. Spending time with your kid is the best investment you could ever make. Not all of us have the money to take our kids to Disneyland, but God in His infinite wisdom, gives Parents, Time, Free. Time to take our children for walks in the park, Time to take drives to look at the Wonders of Mother Nature, as leaves change colors in the Fall. Parents are given Time to teach their children how to throw a football, read a book, and say their prayers. Spend Time taking your children to special events and please, don't miss any events that your children are in. (I've seen many anxious, disappointed faces looking for a familiar face in the audience.)

Make dates with your child. "Nikki, let's go skating, Saturday - just you and me." Do you know how special she feels on these one on one dates? Tune in to your kids and listen to what they're feeling behind the words they say. Find victories - no matter how small. Praise and encourage. Share private little jokes. Tell family secrets. Read to your child - often. Learn your African history, and pass it on to your children, so they will know how courageous their foremothers and forefathers were struggling to open doors that we, today are walking through - doors that must remain open. Education will keep those doors open -

not only for you and your children, but also for all the children of their children. Take your child to the library and instill in him the love of books. Find the Time to give your child "just you and me" Time. Those are memory building times!

And keep your kids busy! Remember that old adage - "Idle hands are the Devil's workshop". In preparation for writing this book, I interviewed several adults who had gone through some troublesome years as they were going through "the Passage" - (their teenage years) . They all wished that their parents had spent more time with them and had found ways to have kept them busy. Find out your children's interests and get them involved in some kind of after - school activity. A lot of churches are opening their doors during the week for such activities, these days. Find out where they are and get your kids involved.

Of course, there are daily and weekly household chores to be done. Get your child in the habit of earning his money. Allowance comes only after chores are done. (And I don't consider the basic making-up bed routine as chores.) Chores can be anything from taking out the garbage, to mopping the floor; just be sure the chores and allowance are age appropriate.

Not too long ago, when I was visiting my son and his family, my son announced that it was "Football Sunday" and he was planning on watching the game on TV Shortly after he had settled in to watch the game, I saw him putting on his coat to go out. I remarked that I thought he was going to watch the game; he simply remarked, "It's more important to play with Maurice"-(his 9 yr. old son). Boy, does he have his priorities in the right place!

I remember MAMA-the name we called my grandmother-(and also the name of a TV show some years ago.) When I was a little girl, my brother and I spent summer vacations with Mama, who lived in a Harlem cold water tenement. Every evening, after supper, (she called it "supper"; we called it "dinner") , she took us for walks. On these walks, she would give us our Instructions for Life. "Always walk in the street like you have someplace important to go - whether you do or not."

"Always wear clean underwear - you never know when you might fall down in the street."

"Speak, so only the person you're speaking to can hear you."

"Remember your table manners - even at home."

And she taught us how to peek through the curtains, so we could see out, without the neighbors knowing we were watching them.

And I remember AUNT VIOLA and the special Easter shopping trips just the two of us would go on - always the day before Easter. Aunt Viola liked flashy clothes, and always looked for hat, handbag, and shoes to match. I was asked to go with her to "help" her pick out her outfit. I was a good little Catholic girl, and always gave up candy and sweets for Lent. Since Lent ended at noon on those Saturdays, we would shop and watch the clock. The minute it turned 12 o'clock, noon, we would rush into a bakery, or five and dime store, and stuff our giggling faces with candy and ice cream the rest of the day. What warm memories I have of those days spent with Aunt Viola!

Love is not enough, Parents! Love without Time is like giving your child a toy without batteries. Give your child your TIME; give your child the BATTERIES of LOVE! Time has a way of flying by. No matter how you spend your time, you will never get that time back. It becomes a memory. Choose to give your child memories of a lifetime!

The TIME that you spend with your child will affect the way he feels about himself. If you're selfish with your time, he will feel he's not worth your time, and therefore, unsure of what love really means. Through all of my teaching years, I could tell within a matter of a few hours, which children came from homes where they were given the Batteries of Love. These children had such a sense of well-being, that no amount of peer pressure could invade their space. These children were respectful, caring, self-disciplined, individuals. These children had better attention spans in the classroom, rarely got involved in fights, and were usually, well liked by their peers.

Remember, Parents, Love comes with a tag - "Batteries Not Included". You must provide the Batteries!

LANGUAGE

*"Speech is the mirror of the soul;
As a man speaks, so is he."*
                              -Syrus

In ancient Africa, and in some other modern cultures, Parents named their children after a family ancestor who had led an exemplary life. The newborn was named with the expectation that he would pattern his life after that of his ancestor. There is the suggestion of vision and expectation in such cultures - don't you think?

"N___!" "B___!" "M___ F___!" We all know what these stand for. Words that once were gut wrenching, are now heard throughout many of our movies, and sung by many of our RAP artists. They're even coming out on T shirts!

For so long, we African Americans have argued against the stereotypical way we were portrayed on the Big Screen by European

American, Hollywood producers. We were either portrayed as big fat Mamas, or subservient buffoons, or slick pimps and hoodlums. African Americans said - "No more of this negative stereotypical stuff! Let's produce our own movies." So we did. Now our movies portray us as slick pimps, hoodlums, drug lords, and whores - (Why is it pronounced "hoe"?) And every other word in the dialogue is "Nigger", "Bitch", with a liberal sprinkling of "M. F. s" and other expletives throughout the movie.

This language caters to the lowest, common element of our society. "That's the way it is in the Hood!" I'm not that far removed from the "Hood" to know that the "Hood" is not entirely this element. They are the loudest and the most obvious, but the majority of the people who live in the "Hood", are decent people, working a 9 to 5, everyday. They are the ones held hostage by the R. A. T. S. of the "Hood".

Do movies imitate Life? Or does Life imitate the movies? I think it's a bit of both -

like a vicious cycle. Think of our kids in this cycle, like show horses going around and around in a circle, with blinders on, so they can't see anything except the rear end of the horse in front of them. You can keep your children out of this cycle by making it quite clear that such language is not acceptable, and neither are such movies. A Brother who calls his Brother a "Nigger" reflects his inner soul. He has internalized the dehumanization and devaluation process that the dominant culture has projected on him. (If I'm a "Nigger", my Brother must be too.) The same internalization is evident every time a Sister calls another Sister a "Bitch".

Violence has become a real part of our world. But to glorify violence in RAP and movies is a betrayal of our people - justified by the money that's made from them. These "R" rated movies are not supposed to be viewed by children under 18, but ask any 10 yr. old if he's seen any of these movies. I guarantee you, most of them will tell you that they've seen them. (I know, because I've asked.) Some of these movies have precipitated violence right inside the theater. And now you find parents bringing these movies right into their homes - via rentals and cable. Even the babies can watch them now!

These movies glamorize violence and crime, drug dealing, and irresponsible sex. (Have you ever seen one of them reach over for a condom in any of the love scenes?) Children are exposed to all of the "glamour" of violence and sex for 2 hours and then in the last 2 minutes of the movie, the bad guy gets killed. Which parts of the movie do you think the kids remember - the first 2 hrs. or the last 2 minutes? Which message do you think they get? When I hear kids say, "That movie was "Bad", do you think there's some psychological reason why their "BAD", means "GOOD"? (But that's another book!)

Parents, it's your responsibility to use the Power of your Hand, by turning the TV control switch to another channel or to Off if you don't like what your child is watching; or the Power of your Voice when you don't want your child to go to see a certain movie. I know you can't protect your child from seeing or hearing things that attack your value system, but you can reduce the amount of violence your child witnesses. (The average child witnesses 200, 000 acts of violence by age 18.) After being immersed in so much violence, your child becomes desensitized to the effects of violence, and will consider the act of picking up a gun and shooting another human being because he was "dissed", a normal, natural reaction. If your child is exposed to scenes or language that attacks the basic values that you're trying to instill into your child, be ready to explain what it means and why it's a negative reflection upon his entire race. Instill upon him that what he says and does is a reflection of his race. And certainly, a reflection on you!

 I remember using the Power of my Hand, when the Three Stooges came on when my children were growing up. Even though it was slapstick, I thought it was just too much repetitive violence. I also remember taking my kids to a movie that I thought was a movie about a haunted house. As it turned out, the movie was about a couple of boys intent on kidnapping some girls and sexually abusing them. When I realized what the intentions of these boys were, I jumped up out of my seat and whispered, "Get up, we're leaving!" When my kids just sat there in stunned disbelief, I repeated a bit louder this time, "Get up , we're leaving!" We laugh now as we look back at that scene - me stalking out of the theater and four kids slinking out behind me, for fear their friends were there and had seen them. It would have been much easier to have let them see the rest of the movie, than have suffered the glaring dirty looks I got on the way home. (They have since seen the entire movie as adults, and admitted that I did the right thing at the time.)

It's much harder to say "No!" than "Yes!", because you have to then deal with, "WHY?" and "Why not?" So many parents are afraid of their children - afraid of making them angry, or afraid of losing their friendship.

Parents, as long as you are responsible for the health, welfare, and safety of your kids, you can not be their Friend. (See the last chapter in this book about the steps you have to take before becoming "Friend".) This fear makes you uncertain and hesitant, and believe me, our kids have built-in antennas that pick up uncertainty and inconsistency and they are ready to attack your weakest point and change it to their advantage. Always be fair. Always be alert for danger. Always be ready to see their side. And never be afraid to say "No!"

Parents, be careful how you use words around and to your children. Be especially careful what you call them. There is no such thing as a "Bad" child - only Bad parenting and Bad teaching. I hear parents say, "He's bad!", as if they're proud of their child's "badness". The child who gets this message will surely try to live up to his reputation and make Mommy proud!

And whatever happened to teaching children courtesy? We teach our children to say "Ta-Ta" for "thank-you" - (Aren't they cute when they're at this stage?) But we have to teach them later on how to give a firm handshake; how to say "Yes, thank-you" and "No, thank-you; how to say "I don't know", instead of shrugging shoulders. And how to present a demeanor that reflects a positive, respectful, attitude.

Give your child the same courtesies you expect from him. "Please" and "Thank-you", are not just "magic" words for children. And always look for opportunities to use words of praise and encouragement - words like, "Good boy!" and "Nice job!" and "Great!" Surprise him by sticking little "love" notes in his lunch kit or book bag that he will find during his day at school, that tells him how proud you are of him.

Language is used to hypnotize. Repetitive mantra-like messages get into the deepest recesses of the mind and can change behavior. Witness the decline in cigarette smoking, since the media campaign has made the image of smoking "uncool". I wonder if the media can begin a campaign against ignorance, bigotry and inequality with the same urgency!

Language is often used to evoke certain feelings in people. Words can be used to encourage and uplift, or they can be used to degrade and humiliate. Words can convince people to buy a certain brand of sneaker, give their lives to the Lord, or plant seeds of hate. Ask anyone who has suffered at the hands of the KKK or the Nazis. A whole mass of people can't enslave millions of people, or round them up in cattlecars bound for ovens, without first planting seeds of hate by dehumanizing them with language. Once the seeds of hate are planted, it becomes easy to take away their human rights and their right to live.

Before the 60's, I , and most other African Americans, would have been offended if someone called us "Black". Indeed, that was just as offensive as being called the "N" word. Then the 60's came along with all of its "Black is Beautiful" and "Black Power" slogans. And we were the first to call ourselves "Black" instead of "Negro". (Isn't Black and Negro the same - only spoken in different languages?)

Black is the color of my hair - (well, it's

more gray now than black.) Black is the color of my favorite dress, and black is the color of a moonless night, but the color of the skin of my people run from the cream colored sands of Egypt to the darkest brown of the cocoa berries in the heartland of Africa. Nowhere's have I seen black skin or white skin. Neither have I seen red skin or yellow skin.

It's time that we stop referring to people by the color of skin and defining them by that and that alone. My six year old nephew, Xavier, once told me that he wished everybody had invisible skin, so we would only see the insides of a person and everybody would look the same. We perpetuate the idea of oppositeness when we refer to Them as "White" and Us as "Black". Both colors are at the opposite ends of the color spectrum.

The color, black, has always been associated with so many negative terms, that it becomes difficult to use it in positive terms. What comes to mind when you hear such terms as "Black Hole", "Black Humor", "Black Monday" -(the day the stock market fell), "Black Clouds -(a sign of stormy weather), "Black sheep of the family," and now there's a new term -"Black ice" -(the ice you don't see that causes people to lose control of their cars.) The one positive term is used when the accountant tells you that your income exceeds your outgo and you're "in the black" as opposed to being "in the red". And I take issue with the print media referring to us as "the blacks"! (with or without a capital "B".)

Using the term "African American", connects us to the large land mass called, Africa. Europeans and Asians refer to their heritage, and the land of their ancestors when they say they are Italian, or Hungarian or Chinese. There is no "Black" History. The history we study is African History, American History, and because the soil of this country and many other countries around the world, holds the blood of our forefathers, African American History. Without African American History, there would be no American History at all!

And when you tell your children that they are both African and American, ask them what each word ends in - I CAN ! I CAN ! That means they CAN twice ! I remember my father taking me to see the Brooklyn Dodgers when Jackie Robinson was playing, after becoming the first "Negro" major league player. My father always reminded me that Jackie couldn't just be good. He had to be TWICE as good. And he had to stay twice as good during his career, to keep the door open, through which many others have followed.

DISCIPLINE

"Don't hesitate to discipline a child. A good spanking won't kill him. As a matter of fact, it may save his life."
—Proverbs, 23: 13, 14.
Good News Bible.

A Parent who gives his child love without discipline, is like a flyer jumping from a plane, without a parachute. The free fall might be exciting, but eventually, there's a price to pay. For the flyer, it's death of the body. For a child it's death of the soul.

A Parent who gives his child discipline without love, inflicts unnecessary pain on his child - and that is unforgiveable. Unforgiveness rots the very lining of the soul and makes a festering sore that never heals.

Discipline allows a child to learn that life has rules and boundaries. It's predictable. A child learns that for every action, there's a reaction - there are consequences. Discipline gives a child a security blanket, but the boundaries must be clear, predictable and consistent. This security blanket will allow him to put his own boundaries in place - (called, self-discipline), and he will be able to withstand the "R. A. T. S." that he will encounter in his daily life as he grows older. The goal of discipline is to convert external forces into internal forces. The goal is self-discipline!

Instilling self-discipline in a child, takes time, energy, constant diligence, and patience. Most of us, I'm sure, were spanked when we were kids. Do you think it did any good? Or do you think it did you harm? (My own children say that it made them - I like to think of it as "molding" them - into what they are today.) Sure, there are thousands of people in the prisons of this country, who were spanked, but there are many, many more good, honest people who were spanked and have never seen the inside of a prison. Some of us are good because we fear the wrath of God. Some of us are honest, because we fear the I. R. S. And some of us are responsible parents because we fear the consequences. A little fear goes a long way. Fear can be a great motivating force against evil. Character is the self-discipline you use when there's no one else around.

I know many of you are gasping right now - (I've heard enough of you on Oprah's show.) "How can you hit your child!" "It's child abuse!" "If you hit your child, you're teaching him to be a hitter." and on and on and on.

Parents, loving God and fearing his wrath, are two sides of one coin. So is the love you've instilled in the heart of your child. Love your child enough to put fear of punishment in his heart too. Whether it be "Time Out" - (most of the kids I talked to said that "Time Out" doesn't work), or taking away privileges - (this sometimes works), or spanking - (this most always works). You notice I say "spanking". There's a big difference between spanking a child and beating a child. Beating is child abuse. Spanking is not. Beating has no rules -

it's harsh and angry and uncontrolled. Spanking has rules; it's swift, immediate and controlled by love. Beating is administered anywhere on the body - sometimes the mind is beaten, sometimes, the soul. Spanking is only administered on the fleshy "seat of knowledge", just enough to reinforce the rule that was broken. Beating is almost always followed by berating, and belittling and makes the child feel hopeless and unworthy of love. Spanking is always followed by discussion, and reassurance that love is unconditional, unwavering and permanent.

When Denise has been told not to leave the yard, and you find her around the corner, it's time for immediate reinforcement of the rules. When Anna brings candy home from the store that she didn't pay for, it's time for immediate reinforcement of the rules. It's better for you to use appropriate methods in the disciplining of your child today, than have the state use their methods, tomorrow.

A responsible parent will eventually be able to reason with a child. If you've been firm and fair, he will understand why you have put restrictions on him. Children reach the age of reasoning at different ages, so you have to be in tuned to your child to recognize when spanking is inappropriate, and serious discussion is in order. By this age your child has built a conscience and knows where the line between right and wrong is.

When I see a child breaking rules without any feelings of guilt, or fear of punishment, I know that a hole grows in his soul - the hole is where his conscience should be. If you recognize a lack of conscience in your kid, don't walk - RUN to your nearest mental health clinic and get help!

To become a doctor, one has to go through Medical School. To become a musician, one has to practice. When it comes to the most important profession in the world - that of Parent - we assume the skills of parenting will come naturally. That might have been true, in the past generation, but in this day when children are having children, another "R", must be added to the curriculum -

Responsibility training. There are sex education courses given, from grade school up, but where is the emphasis on Individual Responsibility? Today's world is not the same as yesterday's world, and I'm sure tomorrow's world will not be the same as today's. You, as a Responsible Parent must be even more alert and on guard - and if you doubt you have the necessary skill, join a Parenting class, or Parent group. If there is none in your area, start one.

As your child grows, so do his responsibilities. Your authority must still prevail, but he must be allowed to make choices, always aware that with choice comes consequence. The concept of "Tough Love" must have come from that old saying - "You make your bed, you lie in it." If you've given him a strong moral immune system, and you've instilled values and self-discipline through the years, have faith in him and his choices. He might put a strain on your rules and your authority, during those rebellious teen years, but don't get discouraged. The teen years are the "Rites of Passage" years. He's searching for that door marked" Independence & Adulthood". When he finds it, your Parental responsibilities end and your mutual friendship begins.

If you're reading this book as a parent of an older child, and recognize that your child has already fallen victim to the R. A. T. S. in your neighborhood, don't despair. You may have to pull the emergency brake on his activities, and try to recover what you both lost, or use more drastic measures, as outlined in the chapter on Solutions.

If you feel deep down in your soul that you have been "Responsibilitating" to the best of your ability, and your child has still gotten swallowed up by the R. A. T. S. , despite all you've done, never give up. Malcolm X changed his attitude and removed the hole in his soul from a prison cell. His Allah removed the hole in his soul. Education changed his attitude. And somewhere there was a parent praying.

SEXUAL RESPONSIBILITY

"A man who creates a baby, and then abandons him, has doomed that baby to play out his life on an unlevel playing field."

Young men! When you allow that 6" protuberance between your legs to control the rest of your body, and you deposit your sperm into a willing vagina without responsibility, you shall neither be called "man" nor "father" if the result is a baby. You shall be called "sperm donor". When you use your penis as a sexual "power trip tool", and your sperm joins with a female egg, you have passed on to that new life the genes of thousands of generations. You are the LINK between the Kings and Queens of Ancient Africa, and the future Kings and Queens of the African Diaspora. Don't let your LINK be the weakest one!

Young ladies! Your body is the Temple that carries the seeds of our NEW AFRICA! Your

Temple is NOT for rent! The Future of our race depends upon you and the seeds of your body. Be sure your seeds stay healthy, strong and Yours until you're ready to share your Temple with another human being. Be selfish with your body. When you allow a boy-child-(more child than boy) to convince you to let him rent your body, all he wants is a warm moist replacement for the hand he's been using in masturbation. If you love yourself, save yourself. Educate yourself, so you and your future children will have a future. Your grandchildren will thank you.

In this day of sexually transmitted diseases, death is a real consequence to unprotected sex. It amazes me that so many children are having children. It's quite obvious that you young people are having irresponsible sex and putting yourselves in grave danger of AIDS.

Our children deserve to be wanted by two parents. It takes the diligence of two parents to protect and defend a child from R. A. T. S. For those of you who can't provide a Father for your child, give your child a Father figure-

be it an Uncle, or Brother, or Friend. If there are no male members in your world to act as a positive male role model, find one in such organizations as Big Brothers or through your religious organization.

It's very important that you do find a responsible man to become a part of your child's life - especially if that child is a boy. The main ingredient that's absent in our young African American boys' lives are Fathers. I am convinced that we African American women cannot successfully, bring our young African American boys through the "Passage" years alone. Once we admit that our power over our young men have its limits, we will be able to turn the reigns of control over to a man before we are forced to turn the reigns of control over to "The Man"!

Single Mothers, when you feel you are losing control of your teenager, consider depositing him on his father's doorstep. This is the most critical time in his life, and he needs a man's hand. This strategy has worked on many of our boys (and girls, too.) It saved my own brother when we were teenagers. After my parents divorced, it became evident that my brother, "Sonny" was showing signs of needing a firm man's hand at the controls, to get him through the "Passage". He later became a Treasury Agent for the U. S. Government, after our family proudly witnessed his graduation from College.

Single Parents, recognize your limits. Admit you need help. Send your child to another environment, if possible. It takes an unselfish, responsible Parent to ask for help. Your child's life is at stake!

But let me assure you single mothers who are struggling to get your child through the "Passage" years, that there are many, many, African American mothers who have brought their boys through all by themselves. Well, they didn't actually do it all by themselves - they had the help of a merciful God. My own Grandmother was one of these women.

Fathers! You have a unique place in the lives of your children. You must always carry yourself with this unique position of yours ever

-present in your mind. No one can be your child's role model, except you. He might admire Michael Jordan or Michael Jackson, but it is not their responsibility to live their lives as your child's role model. Be a "Real Man" and direct his steps through the "Passage" to manhood. If he doesn't have you to show him what it is to be a "Man", he will choose the local drug dealer, to be his "model of a man".

There's an old African proverb: "It takes a whole village to raise a child." Extended families are rare, these days. Extended families mean more than Grandparents, and Aunts and Uncles. Extended families include the people at your place of worship; extended families are your neighbors on the street. If you see my child acting rowdy in the street, it is your responsibility as my neighbor, and her extended family, to correct her, to tell me, and then it's my responsibility as her Parent to communicate my displeasure to her and "reprogram" the computer in her control center.

THANK GOD FOR GRANDMAS! I've said those words so many times during the years that I taught. So many Grandparents find themselves back in the child raising business, for one reason or another. In many cases the parents of the children are drug addicted or in jail. Parents become Grandparents when their teenaged child comes home one day and announces that a baby is on the way. And some of the teenagers are not stopping at one pregnancy. It seems to be "cool" to have babies without benefit of a stable family or the maturity that goes with the responsibility. THIS HAS GOT TO STOP! When you bring a baby into such an environment, you might as well put lead shoes on your baby and expect him to walk. Thousands of these babies are entering the "system" - the Welfare System, the schools, health clinics, hospitals, jails and prisons. Grandparents put all their effort into raising these kids, but they begin to lose stamina and energy as the children grow older.

Grandparents! The fact that you don't want to see your grandchildren suffer, makes you vulnerable for this emotional blackmail. By releasing your children of their responsibility, you are releasing them to continue having irresponsible sex, and more babies. Give your child as much help as you can without taking the total responsibility upon yourself. Make your unwed daughter or son realize that taking Welfare doesn't take their integrity, or their pride, unless they become comfortable in the "system", and make no effort to get out of it.

And for your help, insist that they get some kind of counseling and attend Parenting classes. Give the children of your children as much Grandparenting Love and attention as you can. Let's get a media campaign going that makes having irresponsible sex just as uncool as they have smoking!

Evidently, sex education classes are not the answer. Since schools started sex education classes, the number of teenagers having babies, has skyrocketed. (I always did feel that if you teach a person to fish, or dance, or how to have a baby, that person will be more accepting to the idea of doing it.) I guess for every kid having unprotected sex, there is one using a condom. I have a friend who is a Principal of an inner-city High School. She said that she's not sure whether to be glad or sad, when she sees the back stairwell scattered with condoms.

Parents! Don't let the government be responsible for raising your child ! (They make lousy parents!) Raise your child to be independent. Teach him the facts of Life, when he is 5 or 6 years old. Make your explanations brief and age appropriate. Don't be like the parent who went through the whole explanation of where babies come from, when her 5 yr. old, asked her where he came from. After the long dialogue, he said, "Oh, Ronald and Dane said they came from Chicago!" Parents! Talk to your children honestly about sex. Always be alert and ready to recognize evidence of sexual molestation by other family members, or acquaintances. NEVER put your child in circumstances where sexual molestation is a possibility. And if your child tells you that he has been molested in any way whatsoever, no matter who the person is, for God's sake, believe him! And then take the necessary steps to see that that person never molests another child, again.

Parents who have given their children a "security blanket" of love and discipline; parents who have built up their child's moral immune system, will find , in most cases, a child who has his own sense of self-worth and self-value. And he won't fall for that old Peer Pressure ploy - "Everybody's doing it." If you suspect your child is having sex, deal with it head on. Confront your child and warn him of the dangerous road he is on. If it's your daughter, warn her that the road she's on has two dangerous curves - pregnancy and AIDS! One will interrupt her life; the other will end it!

Just as it was your responsibility to protect your child from being run over by a car when he was six years old, it is your responsibility to protect your child from being run over by sex when he's sixteen years old. For you single working parents, remember, there's no amount of money in this world, that can relieve you of the responsibility of seeing that your child is safe and out of harm's way. I read these stories of parents who took their eyes off of their kid for just a second and in that second, their child was gone - disappeared! kidnapped! You have to be just as alert and watchful when your kid is a teenager. This is not the time to let your guard down.

Single Working Parents! Find yourself a responsible adult to monitor your child's activities after school. A lot of school districts have "after-school" programs for younger children, but there are very few for older children. Therefore, you have to make a decision. Before leaving your child on his own, (remember what I said about idleness being the Devil's workshop?) make your choice:

1) Find a responsible adult to monitor the activities of your child; the friends he has; the problems of his day. A "live-in" is not a choice just for the rich. Many older people would love to be a part of a family. And their responsibilities would be limited only to the

hours that you're not there. I've seen this work in a lot of cases. Or check with the local "Foster Grandparents" Program in your area. They might know someone who's interested in making a few extra dollars. And, of course, you can always invite Grandma to visit for maybe a couple of years - or three - or four!

2) Another choice you have is to cut back your working hours, so that you're home when they get home from school. That way you can be there to praise and encourage when they feel high on accomplishments; or be there to console when they feel low on disappointments and failures. Only a child who has had a parent there for him at these times - when only a parent's praise or consolation would do - can tell you how important this time was.

3) Quit your job, and go on Public Assistance. We all need a helping hand at one time or another. As long as you consider this assistance temporary - just long enough for you to get your child through the "Passage" years. The serious state of affairs in this country - especially, in the African American

communities, is the fact that our children are being abandoned to fend for themselves, with no one spending the time to give them directions. No wonder there are so many "lost" children. It's better for you and your kids to eat "wish" sandwiches - (two pieces of bread and WISH there was something in - between), than to eat steak and wonder where your kids are or who they're with.

4) Get a Home job. I remember my mother sitting at a typewriter for hours, addressing envelopes. She had to work at it 12 to 15 hours a day, seven days a week to make enough money to pay the bills, but she realized the importance of being there to supervise those "Passage" years that my brother and I were going through.

There are hundreds of our children disappearing from our communities every year. Parents, prepare your child for situations that might arise, that might put him in danger. Instruct him what to do under certain circumstances. Play the "what if" game. What if a man approaches him and asks for directions, or asks him to help him look for a lost pet, or help him with a heavy package. What if he's home alone, and Uncle Gil knocks on the door. What if he's home alone and a stranger or a neighbor calls. What if someone comes to his school and tells him that his mother can't pick him up, and he is to go with him. What if - What if - What if.

We can't anticipate every situation, but it's better to be safe than sorry. It's better to make your child cautious and careful, and be able to tuck him in every night, than to be trusting and naive and not know if some child molester is tucking him in . You must be ever watchful and cautious. Teach your child to use his instincts. If he feels uncomfortable about a situation, tell him to follow this rule: "YELL, "NO!", RUN! and TELL SOMEBODY!"

As your children grow and change, so does your Parental role change. You are First, Producer! Then, Teacher, Director, Advisor, Companion, and Friend! Generally in that order, but remember, just as in a football game, you may have to back up sometimes;

you may be pushed back, sometimes, but never give up the struggle to make it to the goal - in this case, the goal is on the 21 year line.

Once you've made a baby, you're THE PRODUCER! - Often referred to as Mother and Father - Parent!

Having produced this "Bundle of Joy", you take on the role of TEACHER! You begin to teach this "bundle of joy" to say "Ma-Ma" and "Da-Da", how to walk, how to hold a fork, and what to do on a potty. You are his first and most important teacher - so you teach him how to write his name, how to hold and read a book, and how to say his prayers.

Then you become DIRECTOR! It's your responsibility as Director to draw up the road map of conduct that directs your child's footsteps. No one gets lost on a straight road, so make it well lit, straight and clear. And lead the way. Educate yourself - your child will follow.

When you become ADVISOR, your child is also going through his Rites of Passage stage. This is the Critical stage, because you will find your own steps a little unsure at times, and you will revert back to the familiar, DIRECTOR role. Try to be a little more objective, be there when advice is needed, and don't take it personally when it's not taken. Adjust the rules as you adjust the child's responsibilities. It's at this point that you'll feel like you're walking a tightrope, because you must still be vigilant and on guard; you must still be in control, and yet you must allow him to test the waters of independence. This is where you do a lot of praying.

If you've survived the last stage, you're ready to be COMPANION! As companion, you will have open ears that listen, open eyes that see, an open heart that feels, and a closed mouth that gathers no feet. Dialogue between you will be honest, and comfortable, sprinkled with humor. And when he makes a decision that fails - (after you told him that it would), whisper this little prayer: "Lord, when I'm wrong, let me admit it; and when I'm right make me easy to live with!"

The FRIEND stage is the BEST! Hang in

there! It's all worth the struggle! Your child has found the Door to Adulthood and Independence! When your child is your friend, you are doubly blessed. In my case I am quadruply blessed, because all of my sons are my friends and my daughter is my best friend. (And I believe I'm hers.) A friend is a person who knows all about you and likes you just the same. Do you like your kid?

SOLUTIONS

Everybody speaks in terms of "shoulds" and "should'ves", when dealing with problems in our communities. Every parent or soon to be parent, put these words out of your vocabulary. Begin THE CHANGE by saying: "IT IS MY RESPONSIBILITY". When you repeat this over and over again, you will begin making a difference inside of yourself. When you change yourself, you change your family. When your family changes, your neighborhood changes. When your neighborhood changes, your schools change. When your schools change, your community changes. When your community changes, your country changes. When your country changes, the world changes. When the world changes, we will have Peace! And it all begins with you!

Start a Parent Advocate Program in your school. Parent advocates will act as the connecting link between parents and teachers;

parents and parents; parents and children; children and children. These parents will be trained to mediate and communicate. These parents will act as a Voice for all of the parents of the school, when rules and regulations are written. And these parents can direct parent "responsibilitating" group discussions in each other's homes. Push for funding for such a program. Until you do, start it as a voluntary effort. It could make a big difference in your school district.

Be a mentor. Adopt a Family. For those of you who have come through the minefield of parenting, successfully, turn around and help another parent in need of "responsibilitating". There's an old African proverb, "Lift as you climb." Be a Foster Grandparent and help guide someone else's child.

Have the courage to speak to young people, when you see them acting up and acting vulgar and rowdy in the street. These kids have put such fear into adults, that they think they can do or say anything and get away with it. And they do! I have gotten out of my car many times to speak to a bunch of rowdy kids. It's all in the way you approach them. If you are intimidated, they will bully you. If you approach them on a one to one, you have a better chance they will listen. And if you speak with quiet, authority, and respect, they may or may not respond the way you would like, but you never know which words you said that will be remembered and make a difference in someone's life. When you throw seeds out on the soil, you never know which will take root and which will not. You might even save a Life!

- Don't be afraid to say "No"!
- Discipline your child.
- Spank! (Only when necessary - followed by a hug and discussion.)
- Insist on Family Meal Time! - Even if it's only once a week.
- Give your child your Time! It's the most precious gift you have.
- Talk to and with your child - Often! And Listen!
- Keep a sense of humor. Laugh a lot!

- If necessary, (and possible), change his environment, (before the State does). Move!

Celebrities! I know you give a lot of your time energy and money to many different causes. Consider establishing farming communities, or wilderness camps for children at risk. Consider taking inner city kids to Africa, where they can spend their "Passage" years, putting all that energy to good use, planting, irrigating, and harvesting the soil of their ancestors. Let them witness children walking miles each day to school, to get whatever education is offered. And take them where they can feed the starving babies. It would be the best education they could ever receive and maybe the life they save will be their own!

MY PLEDGE: I, the undersigned, do hereby promise to contribute part of the proceeds from the sale of this book to any program that sends our African American Students At Risk, to the continent of Africa for their "Passage" years.

LETTER TO GOD:

Dear God,
Thank you for giving me Time; Time to raise four children, through measles and pneumonia; through Honor Roll assemblies and visits to the Principal's Office; through graduations and weddings; through sunny days and stormy days. Thank you for giving me the strength and courage to overcome the "R. A. T. S.", so my children would be able to get their "G. E. D." Thank you for giving me Parents, who instilled a value system inside of me that has been passed on to my children, and they in turn have passed on to their children. Thank you, God, for giving me four children; each one I now call -"FRIEND!"..

"V. C. D."

RESPONSIBILITATING AFRICAN AMERICAN PARENTS

Responsibilitating African American Parents

TO ORDER ADDITIONAL COPIES OF:
"R.A.A.P. - Responsibilitating African American Parents"

1 - Complete order form below
2 - Send $5.95 per book (*plus shipping and handling), Check or Money Order (DO NOT SEND CASH) to:

**SIMOUNTAINHILL PUBLISHERS
BOX 231
LAKE GROVE, NEW YORK 11755**

Please allow 2 - 3 weeks for delivery.
Special school price list available.
Author, **Ida St. Hill**, also accepts speaking engagements for schools and organizations. For more information, please write to above address.

NAME: _____

MAILING ADDRESS: _____

_____

PHONE No.: _____ DATE: _____

QUANTITY_____ @ $5.95 ea. + SHIPPING*_____ =TOTAL_____

*Shipping Charges:

If order totals:	Add:
Up to $9.00	$2.99
$9.01 to $18.00	$3.99
$18.01 to $30.00	$4.99
$30.01 to $45.00	$5.99
$45.01 to $60.00	$6.99
over $60.00	$7.99